WISDOM OF LOVE

Cowrie Divination System

WISDOM OF LOVE

Cowrie Divination System

Laurelei Black

ASTERIA
BOOKS

Wisdom of Love: Cowrie Divination System
By Laurelei Black
Cover Design by Laurelei Black; "Sacred and Profane Love" painting by Titian

ISBN-13: 978-0-9857734-9-6

Copyright 2021

Aphrodites Asterias
Naos
Temple of Starry Aphrodite

Of Cytherea, born in Cyprus, I will sing. She gives kindly gifts to men: smiles are ever on her lovely face, and lovely is the brightness that plays over it.

Hail, goddess, queen of well-built Salamis and sea-girt Cyprus; grant me a cheerful song. And now I will remember you and another song also.

~Anonymous. The Homeric Hymns and Homerica with an English Translation by Hugh G. Evelyn-White. 1914.

For Joe,

who never fails to provide me both
Love and Wisdom.

About the System

Let us start our exploration of this loving, lovely, and (what I hope will become) beloved system of divination with a confession: It is not ancient. It is not a handed-down oracular tradition from maidens in Corinth or wise elders in Cyprus. It is a new divinatory system for ancient Godds.

HOW THIS SYSTEM CAME TO BE

I am a contemporary Priestess of Aphrodite, and as part of the mantic (divinatory/oracular) work I do on her behalf, she gave me the task in 2012 to develop a shell-based system whereby I could perform readings related to issues specifically under her purview. At the beginning, all I knew was that it needed to be shells, and it needed to be some type of cleromancy (lot casting).

As I considered my options, meditated, and talked to other psychic readers, I was asked what I knew of diloggun or the other African diaspora cowrie shell divination systems. At the time, I knew nothing. Even now, not enough to be very knowledgeable. Those systems ARE ancient, and they are lineaged -- meaning authentic practitioners are initiated into traditions by people who have been trained and initiated.

Please know that what I am offering for use in this booklet is NOT a variation of those systems. It is a cleromantic system that utilizes 16 cowries, and that's where the similarities end (to my knowledge). If I stumbled onto any Mysteries from that (or any other system) in my attempt to honor Aphrodite and do as she asked of me, it is genuinely a Divine inspiration.

What happened for me back then was that Aphrodite said, "Yes, the little yoni shells! Those are mine, too. Use those."

Another clue she gave me as I worked on this project was that I should look to geomancy for inspiration, though not too heavily. You'll absolutely be able to see its influence, if you have any familiarity with geomancy -- though once again, it is only a vague influence. What we have in this divination system is something new and wholly aligned to Aphrodisian concerns.

As with the geomantic shapes, our Casting Spreads here are arranged in what I might call "couplets" or pairs. I'm not sure that it's so neatly arranged in geomancy, but in this system, every Spread has its opposite (or partner).

So I got myself 16 cowries, and I held them. I ran my fingers through them. I offered them incense, and I sang to them. I asked them to tell me how they spoke, how they could show me things. It was somewhere around then that they opened their "eyes" and their "mouths." I saw that the rounded sides had rings around them that looked like wide eyes, and the flat sides with the slits could be partially open mouths. These shells could *speak*! They could *see*!

It came to me all at once. A wave of inspiration washing over me. I marked out the patterns of Eyes and Mouths that you see on the following pages, and the meanings of what each of those patterns struck me like a clarion note. It was beautiful! The verses that accompany each pattern poured from me like honeyed wine offered onto the altar. Aphrodite was with me, and the Muses and Graces danced nearby! (Are they laureate-worthy poems? I'd say "no." That isn't their purpose, Dear One. They are there to help you remember and more fully understand the pattern itself. Like a little jingle or ditty.)

READING THE SHELLS

The 16 shells are read in groups of four. (We'll do some sample readings later in the booklet, but let's talk about the basics before we get into the meanings.) There are 16 possible "Eye & Mouth" patterns, and there are 14 possible "Spreads" (meaning shapes that each set of four shells can take).

Your first step will always be to wake up the shells (by shaking them, whispering to them, thanking them, etc -- whatever feels comfortable or makes sense to you) and asking the question on your mind (or your client's). Then you cast the cowries onto a table, mat, cloth, large dish, etc. (You can create something special, if you like. It just needs to be large enough to contain the shells -- and either have a little friction or a lip so the shells don't skitter away and fall.)

You'll be reading all 16 shells, so your second step is to figure out the four groups of four. Before you start interpreting anything about them, just let your mind decide that there are four clusters, and mentally mark them out for yourself.

The final step is interpretation, which is actually many steps rolled into one. When you do a reading, you are interpreting both the patterns and spreads. Both parts will have a meaning for the question that is being asked. As you gain experience, you'll be able to relate the pattern to the spread itself and also to the question -- and then also look for the connections between different parts of the entire reading. It's this interconnectedness that will make your readings supremely potent!

In the beginning, though, it's perfectly fine to take it one piece at a time. (It's even okay to look at this book while you do the reading.)

CONNECTING WITH YOUR COWRIES

Choose your own shells, if you can. Pick them by hand, if at all possible. (If not, it's okay to order them online. Either way, try to get "ring top" cowries, as they are most obviously eyelike.) Offer them incense. Touch them, run your fingers through them, hold them close to your heart. Keep rose quartz, citrine, and/or lapis lazuli in the bag with them. Sing to them. Talk to them. Keep a bottle of Abramelin oil or VanVan oil (or Vervain essential oil) in the bag with them -- which you can sniff prior to doing a reading to get yourself aligned and prepared.

USING THIS BOOKLET

Having been a teacher, I take a "use, lose, abuse" philosophy when it comes to materials. USE what works. LOSE what doesn't.

Twist, contort, cut, stretch (ABUSE) what *almost* works for you until it absolutely works. No tool is useful just sitting on your shelf. So, mark up this book, ignore my suggestions, let the shells offer their own insights. This is a starting place, not the "end-all, be-all."

I placed a few "quick reference" pages right up front that show the Eye & Mouth Patterns and Casting Spreads, without a lot of explanation. Many readers like references like this to help jog their memory regarding the name of a pattern or spread, without getting bogged down in the other material.

Behind these, are another type of short reference, this time for the Eye & Mouth Patterns' accompanying verses. When I created these, I myself found it useful to memorize these verses. On the chance that others might want to do the same, I thought having the verses collected together would make that task easier.

Finally, the most in-depth section of the booklet are the Reflections on each Pattern and Spread. Here, I offer some brief insight into each meaning, and I leave you room to note some of your own thoughts. It's not a lot of room, so you may want a journal for this. The key point is that the *word* associated with the Pattern/Spread is the part I feel was most directly assigned/inspired by Aphrodite -- closely followed by the verse. Let those be beacons as you use this tool and look for your own insights.

QUICK REFERENCE

PATTERNS

LIGHT

 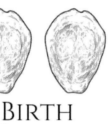

BIRTH

QUEEN OF HEAVEN

 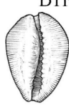 

YOUTH

ENDINGS

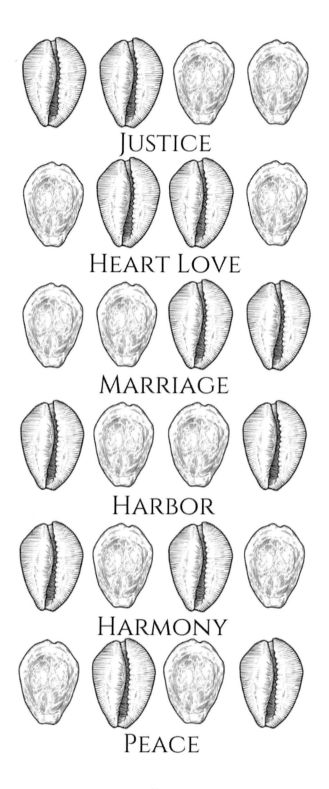

JUSTICE

HEART LOVE

MARRIAGE

HARBOR

HARMONY

PEACE

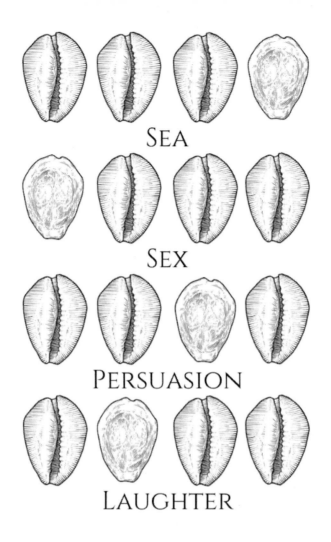

SEA

SEX

PERSUASION

LAUGHTER

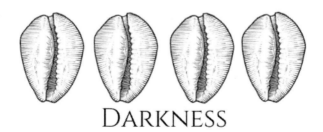

DARKNESS

SPREADS

PATH

HORIZON

JOY

SORROW

MIND

HEART

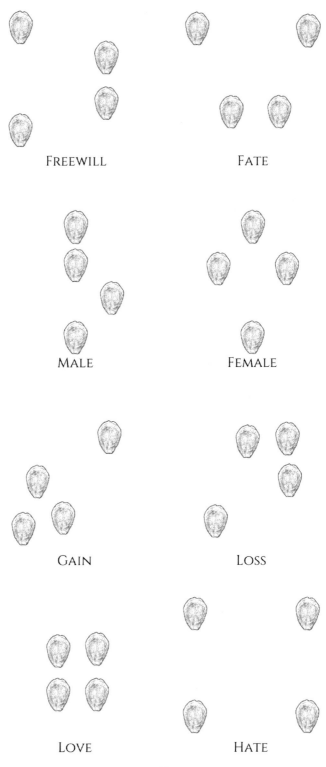

FREEWILL

FATE

MALE

FEMALE

GAIN

LOSS

LOVE

HATE

VERSES & REFLECTIONS

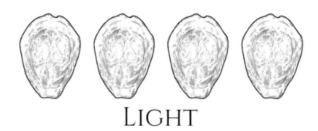

LIGHT

You're not worthy, and yet you ARE
both earthbound mud and shining star.
Arise and go into the night
to see, to BE the guiding light.

Aphrodite is a starry Goddess. She's associated with the planet Venus
-- the Evening Star, the Morning Star. She's credited with being a
navigator and a helper to sailors on the deep sea. She can be your
navigator and helper, as well. She is a bridge between Sky and Sea,
and she reminds us that we, too, are star-stuff -- wrapped in humble
earth, though we may be. This pattern is often that reminder that
however dark the night around (or within) us is, we carry Divine Fire.
Let it shine, Dear One! Someone needs their lamp lit.

Also take note that this is the beginning of the patterns. All watchful,
shining, golden-ringed eyes. Keep your eyes open! Look for signs of
hope and wonder. (They will likely be quiet, even if they are right out
in the open -- in broad daylight.)

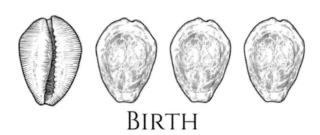

BIRTH

In blood and soil and toil and pain
you're born into this world again.
From cauldron-womb to mother's breast,
your journey starts; you cannot rest.

Birth and new beginnings are full of bright promise, but they can also be hard -- on both mother and child. This pattern reminds you that there is comfort in the motherly side of doting Aphrodite, if we think of her relationships with Aeneas, Harmonia, Eros, etc. However, even she can't entirely shield you from the hardships associated with your choices -- or life's work.

QUEEN OF HEAVEN

Evening star, the Queen of Heaven,
Passing through the trials, seven.
The Hero or the Fool we are,
rising like the Morning Star.

You are on the Mythic Journey. Maybe you even recognize some aspect of it -- the Road of Trials, the Belly of the Beast, Confronting the Shadow. If you are at the beginning of this journey, you may be like the Fool, unaware as yet where you're headed or what the quest involves -- or what perils are in store. If you're further along the road, you may be actively striving to earn the title of Hero -- integrating wisdom, integrating the Self.

Those obstacles and foes who are constantly foiling your plans? They are the Guardians of the Mysteries you must face. They aren't your real enemy. You are.

Your goal is not to slay the Queen of the Underworld, my love. Your goal is to know and love her as your Sister. As your Self. Until you do it -- beyond lip service -- she'll have you trapped. Psyche on the slab. Ishtar on the hooks.

YOUTH

An ancient and undying Truth:
Each age conceals an inner youth.
Remaining young is not an art.
Hold your youth within your heart.

Aphrodite was honored as *Ambologera* -- She Who Postpones Old Age -- in ancient Greece. Even the Ancients had concerns about growing old that, I imagine, were rooted in something deeper than vain conceit. Youth isn't just about looking young. It's also about feeling young and being able to physically do things for both enjoyment and survival. While families in traditional cultures have typically taken care of their elders better than contemporary society does, that doesn't mean that every individual had that kind of security.

The youth referenced in this pattern, though, refers less to the physical body and more to the mental and psychological outlook of the individual. Hope, humor, cheer, a carefree nature, and a future -facing perspective are the hallmarks of the young. Holding onto these qualities is a way to keep a Fountain of Youth bubbling.

ENDINGS

All roads, all days, all songs must end
to sleep, to breathe, begin again.
A treasure's hid in sorrowful endings:
the promise of a new beginning.

Some aspect of your query is approaching a place of closure. Your wisest course of action is to choose to be at peace with this inevitable ending. This isn't to say that your feelings of pain or sorrow (if you have them) are invalid. Feel what you feel, and move through your uncomfortable feelings at your own pace. This full-cycle integration allows you to move naturally into Whatever Is Next without holding onto the past in damaging ways.

It's worth noting that this ending may not be a total cessation of the target circumstance or relationship of the reading. It might just mean some part of it is coming to a close. Look to other parts of the reading for more information.

JUSTICE

Justice, with her scales and sword,
measures both your deed and word.
Intents and thoughts she does not weigh.
Be careful what you do and say.

The planet Venus rules the astrological sign of Libra, the scales. Those scales are said to be held by Virgo, the starry Virgin; but once, long ago, the stars of Libra were considered to be Scorpio's claws. In this trio of signs, we see reminders of Lady Justice, ready to take the measure of our impact on the world -- and mete out punishment or praise, as earned.

There is a warning here, when this pattern presents itself. Your heart may be in the right place, but that only goes so far, my love. We are held accountable for our speech and actions.

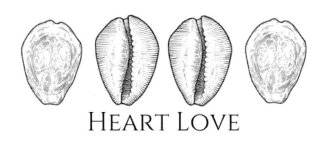

HEART LOVE

Love of mother, love of son.
Love deeply and love everyone.
Love friends and children and your mate.
Love till there is no room for hate.

When we look at Aphrodite's relationships, we see she is a doting mother, a faithful friend, and a passionate paramour. Her relationship with her husband, Hephaestus, is complicated -- at least, as described by Homer. But I have long maintained (and written elsewhere) that Aphrodite loved and was passionate about him, as well. Indeed, they had an Alchemical Marriage (star maiden and metalsmith, Ocean-born Goddess and Volcano-cast God).

Love, in this pattern, is a verb, not a noun. You are being called to step up your love game. DO love. MAKE love. BE love.

MARRIAGE

Sacred Union – hearts and minds,
bodies, lives, and souls entwined –
Bless each one with joy and pleasure.
Such a gift is priceless treasure.

There is a deep and intimate connection here. The "marriage" in this pattern doesn't have to reference any sort of civil or legal union, but it absolutely signifies a long-term connection on multiple levels. This is a partnership, a relationship. In a best case scenario, everyone is getting what they need and is looking toward the future with a hopeful eye.

HARBOR

Safe within a an earthen shield,
unruly seas to harbors yield.
Anchored firmly in this calm
your bark escapes the threat of harm.

What is your safe place? It might be time to go there -- or time to recreate aspects of it where you are now. The shells are letting you know that this is a time when you need the safety of the harbor. Look around. It may already have manifested itself around you in some way. Have your guardians and protectors strategically positioned themselves to act as a shield? They may sense danger on your periphery.

Harmony

Bless'd accord, cooperation.
No thought of ire or base frustration.
Heads and hearts in loving ease.
Home and self have found some peace.

It feels so nice not to have to argue or walk on eggshells. Maybe you haven't felt that in a while, but the shells say it's either here or on its way. That sense of mutually beneficial cooperation with those around you -- those closest to your question. What a beautiful environment of loving energy! It's easy to understand that Harmonia was Aphrodite's daughter.

PEACE

Dove of Peace, we draw you near.
Take from us both pain and fear,
leaving only your sweet love
to live in peace, O Gentle Dove.

Eireine (Peace) and Colomba (Dove) are two of Aphrodite's epithets. The gentle dove is seen as an emblem of both personal and cultural peace in societies around the world, right up to modern day. Whether your query involves tumult, anxiety, fear, grief, or pain, let the Dove of Peace approach. She is signaling her proximity by showing up in this reading.

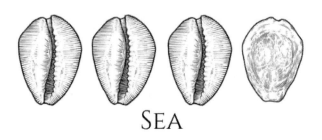

SEA

Open waters, clear and bright,
Sky-kissed ocean brings delight.
Dark below, as any tomb.
Mother Ocean, life's great womb.

The sea itself is Aphrodite's mother, and is mother to all life on earth. Brimming with life and beauty, fun and sun on its surface, it is also a dark, mysterious, and unfathomable depth with its own secrets, tempests, and terrors. What or who, in your query, is bigger and more powerful than you might be giving it (or them) credit for? What might have a side you can't plumb or had never considered? It's time to consider the unknown, my love. It is certainly considering you.

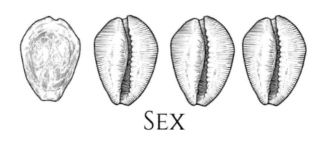

SEX

Sacrament of love divine,
bliss-filled bodies intertwined.
In best of cases, spirits mesh
while taking joy in earthly flesh.

Sexual union is a Divine Sacrament (when it occurs between enthusi-astically consenting adults) because it allows us to connect deeply with our Selves, with the Beloved Other (when present), and with the Divine. Alchemical Union can transpire between people connected in this sacred act. Gnosis can happen. Does it always? Nah. But it *can*, and that makes it a gift from the Divine. An Aphrodisian Sacrament.

These shells LOVE to talk about your sex life. Whether you're having mystical sex, purely entertainment-value sex, fantastic write-blogs-about-it sex, or terrible see-a-therapist-about-it sex, these shells are going get chatty about this topic early and often.

PERSUASION

Silver speech and golden belt
can cause the Will of All to melt.
Hold convictions, tight and true,
or watch them charmed away from you.

Aphrodite had a daughter called Persuasion, and it was also an epithet used of Aphrodite herself. When the Golden Goddess wore her golden belt (a double sash that criss-crossed her heart), nobody could refuse her.

Someone is trying to charm the pants off of you. Maybe literally. Maybe figuratively. It's time to take stock of your convictions and ethics regarding this query. You need to know where you stand because somebody involved has an agenda, and they are good at getting what they want. Before you give in, make sure you are in alignment, or you'll regret it later.

LAUGHTER

Pleasure, joy, and untamed bliss,
delight and humor, marked by this.
Bubbling font from Spirit's well.
Laughter in your Soul does dwell.

Real laughter is healing for the soul and for the body. In Attic Greek,
the words for laughter-loving and genital-loving are almost identical
-- and both are used as epithets for Aphrodite. I maintain that this is
because genitals are hilarious. I've also read, though, that laughter
and smiling was anciently (and is still contemporarily) seen as sensu-
al and erotic. Ever had the giggles during lovemaking? Ever been
turned on by someone's laugh? We are put at ease by humor, and we
are able to relax into our sexuality and sensuality thereby. There's
also interesting research regarding the vagus nerve, which connects
-- among other things -- the vocal cords, the uterus, and the genti-
alia. Intense vocalizations of all sorts, including laughing, yelling, and
singing, can then cause sexual arousal. Laughter AND genital loving,
indeed!

Get some chuckles, love. They're good for your whole body.
They're good for your heart and soul.

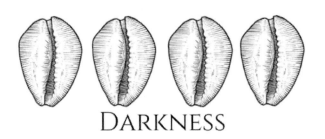

DARKNESS

No light or slim reflection cast.
The door is sealed shut, firm and fast.
Within the blackest pitch of night,
Embrace the Dark and mourn the Light.

Aphrodite has a few epithets that point to her nature as a Goddess that can guide us through dark times and help us embrace and understand our Shadow -- Epitymbia (She of the Tombs), Melaina (Dark), and Skotia (Black). Some scholars feel that the references to darkness and blackness are because her deeds (namely, sex) are done under cover of night. Maybe so. But what of Epitymbia? The short version is that Aphrodite is not just a Goddess of celestial light and all things golden. She teaches us to mourn deep loss (as she herself does when Adonis dies). She teaches us to move through the darkness of the Underworld (as she sends Psyche to do).

This pattern acknowledges the mourning and grief within us and cautions us not to search for a candle until we have taken the time to know our darkness. If we shove it to the side too quickly, it will come back later -- with teeth and claws.

SPREADS

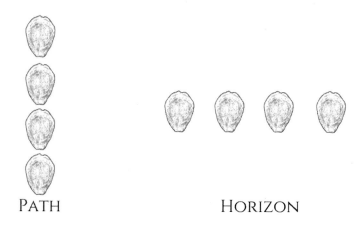

PATH   HORIZON

The Path speaks of the journey ahead of you, your life's course, or the long road. It tends to speak to a long view of events, things further in the future, or dealing with the scope of time.

The Horizon speaks of new vistas just over the next hill, milestones, and rites of passage. It tends to suggest events coming up soon.

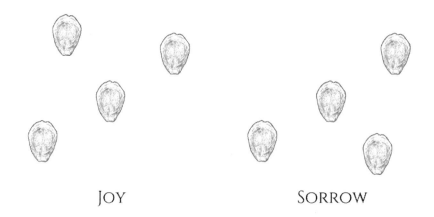

JOY   SORROW

Joy and Sorrow are a soaring dove and falling dove, respectively. Joy is uplifted, reaching for new heights, free to play and sing. Sorrow is wounded, stooping, dropping to earth with the weight of a stone.

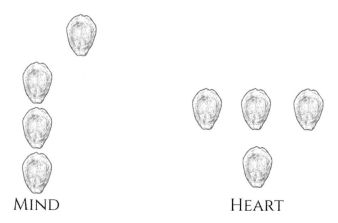

MIND   HEART

These spreads let you know where the question is really coming from. Is this a dilemma of the mind or of the heart? Sometimes the answer isn't as obvious as we think at first glance.

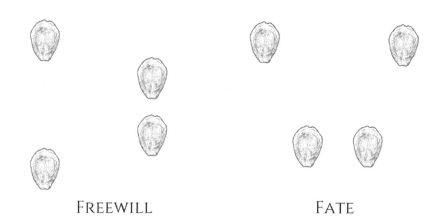

FREEWILL   FATE

These spreads represent a dice cup -- upright and overturned. The upright cup holds your fate, your luck, your destiny. Not all things are decided, but all possibilities are contained in the sacred vessel, and certain outcomes are more likely in this potent time. Overturned, your choices around this issue hold more sway than at other times. Choose carefully.

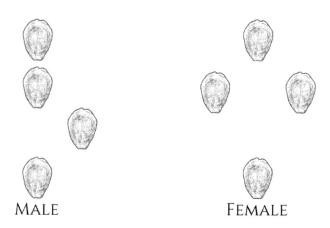

MALE   FEMALE

These figures represent a person who identities as a man, and a person who identifies as a woman. They will likely be someone known to the querent -- or someone about to enter their life.

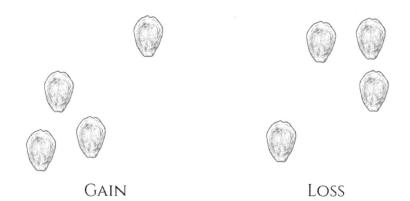

GAIN   LOSS

These spreads represent the fluctuation of the scales. Remember that we read these figures from left to right, so you'll be reminded when you see only one cowrie on the left side of the scales that this means "loss" or "less." Three on the left is "gain" or "greater."

LOVE   HATE

Love is a coming together of forces -- of all types of forces in the universe. It is a binding together. A union.

War is a wrenching apart. It is strategic and tactical division. It is isolation.

SAMPLE READINGS

For the sample readings included here, I've provided two pictures of each reading. The first shows the shells without marking or identification, just as they fell into the tambourine (my preferred reading dish). Seeing them this way allows you, as a student of the shells, to get your own impressions of their messages without having my vision imposed upon them.

The second picture is an identical photograph in every way, except that I have marked out the spreads *as I interpreted them.* I make the distinction here that this is *my personal read* of these spreads because (as I think you'll quickly discover) there is room for individual interpretation. You will develop your own unique relationship with your shells. They will speak to you differently than mine do with me. Like lovers or closest confidantes, they will whisper to you, wink at you, and sing their songs in a special cadence just for you, and that communication will be subtle and unique.

You'll notice that only one of the three sample readings has to do with love, relationship, sex, beauty, etc (ie, those things typically considered within "Aphrodite's domain"). I mentioned in the first few pages of this booklet that these shells have a real talent for offering guidance and illumination in these areas, and they do! I included readings in other spheres of influence, though, to illustrate both the shells' and Aphrodite's versatility in addressing concerns related to a myriad of areas. Aphrodite is both earthly and heavenly. She is of the sea and the sky. Anciently, she was honored by magistrates and officials of high rank throughout the political and military sphere, and she was a Goddess of home and family -- bringing harmony, peace, and a beautiful life. She held influence from the cradle to the grave, in both public and private life. Truly, ask Her about anything!

I hope that by sharing the following readings, I am able to open up a pathway or dialogue for you as you start talking with your shells.

Question: What does the querent need to know about housing and home prospects at this time? (Querent was considering moving into a new home.)

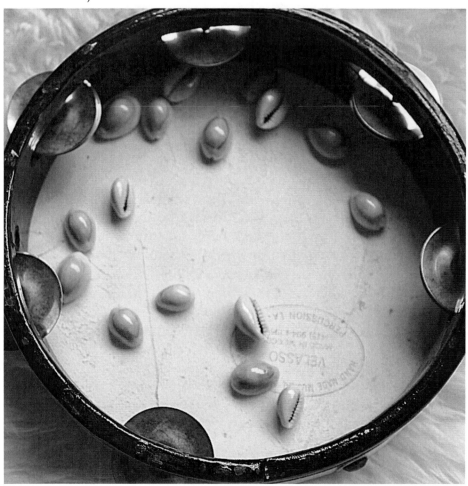

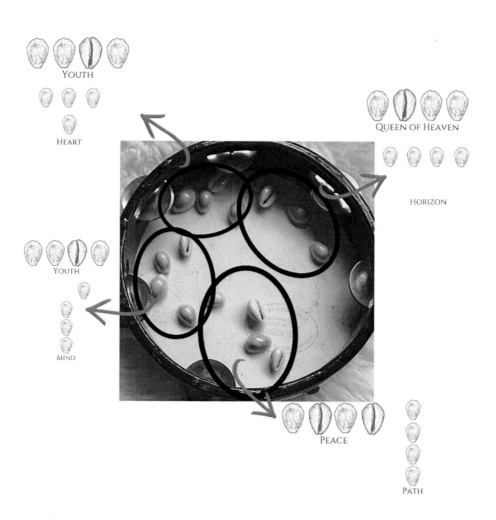

YOUTH

HEART

YOUTH

MIND

QUEEN OF HEAVEN

HORIZON

PEACE

PATH

47

Question: What does the querent need to know about housing and home prospects at this time? (Querent was considering moving into a new home.)

This is how I saw the message in the shells:

Youth—Heart

Youth—Mind

Queen of Heaven—Horizon

Peace—Path

The idea of a new residence is a hopeful one for the querent, but it is an idea in its infancy right now. It is a question that lives very presently in the mind and heart, but it isn't fully formed or ready to be acted upon yet. There may be a sense of impatience and frustration around not getting to move forward at this time.

The maturation of this desire is on the horizon, says the Queen of Heaven, though the process may be one of overcoming obstacles along the way.

In the long run, there will be peace on the subject (and in the home). Contentment.

Question: The querent is going through a difficult time in her romantic relationship. She feels ending things may be the best course of action.

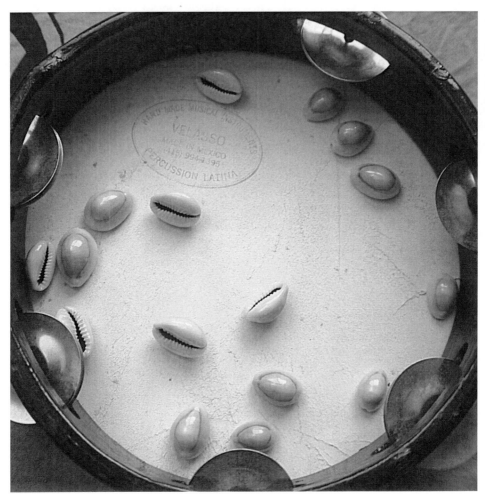

SEA

FEMALE

BIRTH

MIND

JUSTICE

HEART

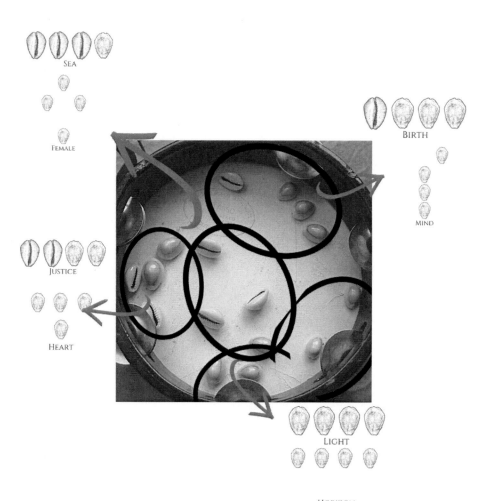

LIGHT

HORIZON

Question: The querent is going through a difficult time in her romantic relationship. She feels ending things may be the best course of action.

This is how I saw the message in the shells:

Sea—Female

Justice—Heart

Birth—Mind

Light—Path

The querent has strong ties with the Sea — and with a Sea Goddess. (Not Aphrodite — and not one most people associate with the Sea.) She carries the tides inside her, and those tides are shifting in a powerful way. The Sea Goddess is present with and offering guidance to the querent.

Where issues of Justice come up regarding the Heart, there is often a terrible price for someone to pay for their misdeeds. Someone's heart, someone's loyalty are being measured and weighed in what is likely a significant reckoning. It is prudent for the querent to judge both the actions and speech of her partner for what they are, and to take the advice herself that she would give a friend in the same situation.

The querent is at the beginning of this process — a new birth of a new Self. A new way to understand herself, to know herself. The change she is considering is one that speaks to her very identity. She would be moving from "We" to "I" — after a long time as "We." She needs to be gentle and nurturing with the new "I."

In the long run, the process she is undergoing will be for the best for her. What she is going through now will create light within her and around her.

Note: I'm always very cautious about telling a querent: "Yes, do this" or "No, don't do that." Instead, as a general guideline, I let them know that the shells (or other reading tool) are giving them a picture of how things stand based on current circumstances.

In a reading like this, the shells (and the Power behind them) are speaking to how things are and could be if the querent continues moving in a trajectory of "ending things." To get another perspective, we could have cast the shells again and asked, "What should the querent anticipate if the relationship continues?"

SAMPLE READING 3

Question: Querent desires a quick "life path" check-in.

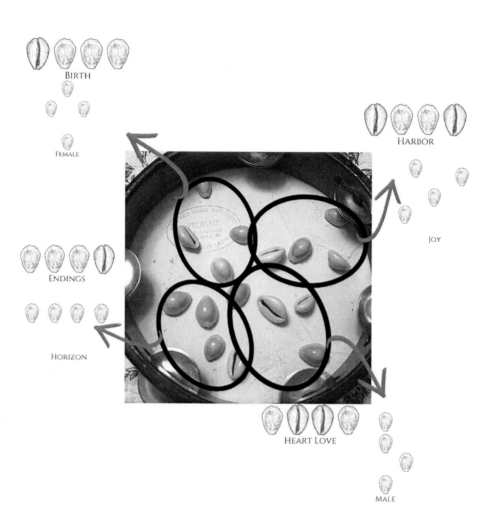

BIRTH

FEMALE

HARBOR

JOY

ENDINGS

HORIZON

HEART LOVE

MALE

SAMPLE READING 3—INTERPRETATION

Question: Querent desires a quick "life path" check-in.

This is how I saw the message in the shells:

Birth—Female

Endings—Horizon

Harbor—Joy

Heart Love—Male

The querent is going through a new phase in her journey as a woman. Something about her physical being or her sense of self. Maybe a deep contemplation of what it means to be a "woman" brought on by the end of one phase or cycle and the beginning of another.

This feels tumultuous and challenging, to have both beginnings and endings mentioned so specifically in close succession. We know they happen that way, but to have them made so obvious really points out the stress of the situation.

There is joy and comfort and hope in a sanctuary, though. The querent needs to turn to safe space (either ideologically or physically). Create or find retreat space. Go into a chrysalis for this transformation at hand.

And the querent can take comfort and strength in the male ally with whom she shares such deep love. That love will be a touchstone throughout this journey.

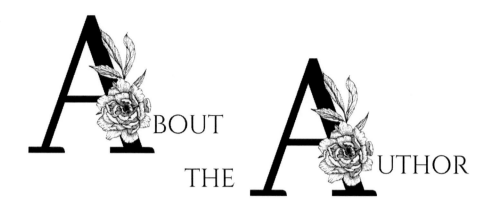

ABOUT THE AUTHOR

Laurelei Black is a hedge-rider, a Cunning Woman, a traveler on the crooked path. She is a priestess of love and pleasure, an Ishtar-woman, an Aphrodite-woman. She is a friend to daemons and a mate to the Red God. A bone collector; a temple dancer. Laurelei is the author of 13 books (including *Temple of Love* and *The Witches' Key to the Legion: A Guide to Solomonic Sorcery*), a co-Director and frequent presenter at the **Babalon Rising Festival**, an OTO initiate, a co-owner of **Camp Midian**, and the proud proprietress of **Asteria Books and Events** and of **Blade & Broom**.

Laurelei began serving Aphrodite in 1999 while she was living in Los Angeles and working with with a Traditional Witchcraft (aka "European Pre-Christian Religious Traditions") coven. She became a priestess to Aphrodite within that religious tradition when she took her 2nd Degree, in 2002.

In addition to her work as a Priestess of Aphrodite, Laurelei is a Cunning Woman, a Wise Woman of the traditional path. She and her ex-wife, Natalie, founded the American Folkloric Witchcraft tradition, where Laurelei continues to explore the convergence of American magic and traditional British craft. Within this realm, Laurelei's keenest interests include ancestor work, bone collecting, and potion-making.

Laurelei is the author of four books devoted to Aphrodite's worship, including *Cult of Aphrodite* (a compilation of well-researched rituals and religious festivals in Her honor); *Crown of Violets* (a book of devotional poetry and art); *Temple of Love* (a historical novel depicting the poet Sappho as an Aphrodite Priestess); and *Aphrodite's Priestess* (a resource book for those who would serve Love).

Laurelei has also offered the Witchcraft community the Red Thread Academy (a complete Traditional Witchcraft education), *Liber Qayin*, a channeled gospel (co-authored by Natalie Black); *The Witches' Key to the Legion: A Guide to Solomonic Sorcery*; the Asteria Mystery School (a magickal learning library); and the Asteria Books' *Book of Shadows* printable PDFs (a vast collection of about 730 individual pages -- and growing) available through Blade & Broom on Etsy.

Laurelei continues to write, teach, speak, and coach. She lives in Kentucky with her family.

Check out her work via <u>linktr.ee/laureleiblack</u>

Made in United States
North Haven, CT
27 October 2021